MARY KATE AND ASHLEY OLSEN

A Real-Life Reader Biography

Kathleen Tracy

Mitchell Lane Publishers, Inc.

P.O. Box 619
Bear, Delaware 19701

Second Printing

Real-Life Reader Biographies

Paula Abdul	Christina Aguilera	Marc Anthony	Lance Armstrong
Drew Barrymore	Jan & Stan Berenstain	Tony Blair	Brandy
Garth Brooks	Kobe Bryant	Sandra Bullock	Mariah Carey
Aaron Carter	Cesar Chavez	Roberto Clemente	Christopher Paul Curtis
Roald Dahl	Oscar De La Hoya	Trent Dimas	Celine Dion
Sheila E.	Gloria Estefan	Mary Joe Fernandez	Michael J. Fox
Andres Galarraga	Sarah Michelle Gellar	Jeff Gordon	Mia Hamm
Melissa Joan Hart	Salma Hayek	Jennifer Love Hewitt	Faith Hill
Hollywood Hogan	Katie Holmes	Enrique Iglesias	Allen Iverson
Janet Jackson	Derek Jeter	Steve Jobs	Michelle Kwan
Bruce Lee	Jennifer Lopez	Cheech Marin	Ricky Martin
Mark McGwire	Alyssa Milano	Mandy Moore	Chuck Norris
Tommy Nuñez	Rosie O'Donnell	**Mary-Kate and Ashley Olsen**	Rafael Palmeiro
Gary Paulsen	Colin Powell	Freddie Prinze, Jr.	Condoleezza Rice
Julia Roberts	Robert Rodriguez	J.K. Rowling	Keri Russell
Winona Ryder	Cristina Saralegui	Charles Schulz	Arnold Schwarzenegger
Selena	Maurice Sendak	Dr. Seuss	Shakira
Alicia Silverstone	Jessica Simpson	Sinbad	Jimmy Smits
Sammy Sosa	Britney Spears	Julia Stiles	Ben Stiller
Sheryl Swoopes	Shania Twain	Liv Tyler	Robin Williams
Vanessa Williams	Venus Williams	Tiger Woods	

Library of Congress Cataloging-in-Publication Data
Tracy, Kathleen.
    Mary Kate and Ashley Olsen/Kathleen Tracy.
        p. cm. —(A real-life reader biography)
    Summary: A biography of the teenaged twin sisters who began their acting careers at the age of nine months in the television series "Full House;" became producers and stars of their own videos, CDs, and books; and have recently started a clothing line and magazine.
        Includes index.
    Filmography: p.
    ISBN 1-58415-124-2 (library binding)
    1. Olsen, Ashley, 1986—Juvenile literature. 2. Olsen, Mary-Kate, 1986—Juvenile literature. 3. Actors—United States—Biography—Juvenile literature. [1. Olsen, Ashley, 1986- 2. Olsen, Mary-Kate, 1986- 3. Actors and actresses. 4. Women—Biography.] I. Title. II. Series.
    PN2287.O36 T73 2003   2002022124

ABOUT THE AUTHOR: Kathleen Tracy has been a journalist for over twenty years. Her writing has been featured in magazines including The Toronto Star's "Star Week," *A&E Biography* magazine, *KidScreen* and *TV Times*. She is also the author of numerous biographies including "The Boy Who Would Be King" (Dutton), "Jerry Seinfeld - The Entire Domain" (Carol Publishing) and "Don Imus - America's Cowboy" (Carroll & Graf). She recently completed "The Complete Idiot's Guide to Portrait Photography" for Alpha Books.

PHOTO CREDITS: cover: Ben Strauss/Shooting Star; p. 4 Tom Rodriguez/Globe Photos; p. 10 ABC/Kobal; p. 17 Judie Burstein/Globe Photos; p. 18 Mitzi Trumbo/Shooting Star; p. 21 Randy Harmon/Shooting Star; p. 22 Eric Liebowitz/Kobal; p. 25 Andrea Renault/Globe Photos

ACKNOWLEDGMENTS: The following story has been thoroughly researched, and to the best of our knowledge, represents a true story. While every possible effort has been made to ensure accuracy, the publisher will not assume liability for damages caused by inaccuracies in the data, and makes no warranty on the accuracy of the information contained herein. This story has not been authorized nor endorsed by Mary-Kate or Ashley Olsen.

Table of Contents

Chapter 1   You "Musta" Been Beautiful Babies 5

Chapter 2   Full House 9

Chapter 3   Home Away from Home 14

Chapter 4   A League of their Own 19

Chapter 5   Changing with the Times 24

Chronology 28

Filmography 29

Index 32

Chapter 1
You "Musta" Been Beautiful Babies

Many successful actors will tell you that they grew up dreaming of being performers. Then they spent years working and studying toward making that dream come true. But there are a few who literally grew up being performers, such as Mary-Kate and Ashley Olsen. Before they were even a year old, the outgoing sisters were starring in a popular television series. By the time they were in first grade, the Olsens were the most popular child performers since Shirley Temple—and they show no signs of slowing down.

Ashley Olsen was born on Friday, June 13th, 1986. Contrary to superstition, the day turned out to be especially lucky for proud parents David and Jarnie Olsen. Just a few

Before they were a year old, Mary-Kate and Ashley Olsen were starring in a TV series.

minutes after Ashley came into the world, Mary-Kate was born. Even as infants, the sisters looked strikingly alike even though they are not identical twins. They are fraternal twins, regular siblings who just happen to be born at the same time.

The Olsen family, which also included Mary-Kate and Ashley's older brother Trent, lived in an area of Los Angeles called Sherman Oaks. Nestled near the foothills that surround the San Fernando Valley, Sherman Oaks is only a few minutes' drive away from television and movie studios. Although many people in the area work at the studios, neither David nor Jarnie Olsen was "in the business" when their children were born. David was a mortgage banker and Jarnie, a former dancer with the Los Angeles Ballet, was a stay-at-home mom. The idea of Mary-Kate and Ashley becoming television stars was the last thing on their parents' minds.

But that all changed the day Jarnie went shopping with a friend, a woman whose child was pursuing an acting career. On the way home, the woman needed to stop by the office of her child's talent agent. When Jarnie mentioned that she had twin daughters, the agent immediately asked to see pictures of the girls. After one look, he wanted them to

The Olsen family lived in Sherman Oaks, California, just a few minutes' drive from television and movie studios.

audition for an upcoming television series about a widowed dad raising his three young daughters. One of the girls was a toddler. Because of laws limiting the number of hours that very young children can work, producers often look for twins who can share the role. That way, each child only has to take on half the workload.

Although Jarnie really didn't believe Mary-Kate and Ashley would get hired, she decided to go on the audition anyway because it seemed like fun. The scene inside the casting office was loud and chaotic. Dozens of twin sisters were crawling all over the room. It looked more like a nursery than a TV show office. Many of the twins already had professional experience, either in television series or commercials. But for Mary-Kate and Ashley this was just an amazing new adventure as the little girls waited for their turn.

The series being cast was called *Full House* and stand-up comedian Bob Saget was already set to be the dad. Mary-Kate and Ashley were auditioning for the role of Michelle, the baby of the family. To Jarnie's utter disbelief, the girls were hired on the spot.

The scene inside the casting office was loud and chaotic. Dozens of twin sisters were crawling all over the room.

The girls, then just seven months old, "were unique," said the new show's executive producer, Robert Boyett. "They had big, expressive eyes. They were friendly and would listen when you spoke to them."

Even so, David and Jarnie considered the whole thing a fluke. They never expected their daughters' "career" to last much more than a few months because the chances of any new television show becoming a hit are very low. And that certainly seemed to be the case with *Full House.* It got terrible reviews and not many people watched it. Jarnie assumed the show would be canceled after the first season. She was grateful for the money Mary-Kate and Ashley earned and put it into a savings account the girls could use when they were older. She figured that their lives would soon be getting back to normal.

But things didn't work out that way. As the weeks went by, more and more people became regular viewers of *Full House.* By the end of its first season, it was on its way to becoming one of the most popular comedies on television. And for Mary-Kate and Ashley, the excitement was just beginning.

Chapter 2
Full House

The twins were still just nine months old when the pilot episode of *Full House* was made. The series began its regular filming even before the girls had celebrated their first birthday. Although the idea was to use the toddlers equally, it ended up that TV viewers saw Mary-Kate almost exclusively in the beginning. That was because Ashley would start crying every time she was set in front of the camera.

A turning point came later in the season when Mary-Kate developed a sty. The producers had to rely on Ashley when shooting day came around. But this time, Ashley performed like a pro and everyone was thrilled. It just took Ashley longer to adjust to her new surroundings and get

The series began regular filming before the girls were a year old.

The cast of **Full House** *is pictured: left to right: Dave Coulier, Jodie Sweetin, Mary-Kate Olsen, Bob Saget, Candace Cameron, Lori Loughlin, and John Stamos.*

comfortable with the noises and busy activity of a working television set. Once she did, she was every bit as adorable on film as Mary-Kate was, although their styles were different.

"Mary-Kate is more serious, so she got to do the serious lines," said Jarnie. "When they needed someone to be more active or emotional, they let Ashley do it."

In fact, the sisters were so professional and such natural performers that they avoided the usual fate of most baby and toddler actors. Quite often, a long-running series that features very young children will have the child age quickly from one season to the next, then recast the role with an older child actor. Part of the reason is economic—it is cheaper to pay one young actor than two. But the producers of *Full House* decided to let the character of Michelle grow up in "real time." Fans of the show got to watch her develop from diapers to her first steps to her first words and then into childhood—week after week after week. This is one reason why she was so popular.

Once the twins got old enough so that one or the other could have easily handled the workload by herself, the producers made an even more unusual decision. They decided to let Mary-Kate and Ashley continue to share

In the beginning, Mary-Kate was seen more on the show because Ashley would cry every time she was in front of the camera.

the part. For one thing, the cast and crew loved the Olsen girls so much that the idea of choosing one over the other to stay with the show seemed heartless.

But there was another reason for keeping both of them. The twins had a loyal following of fans. The producers worried about a backlash against the show if one of the girls was let go in favor of the other. So both girls stayed and shared the role of Michelle for the series' entire eight-year run.

Like the Olsens, most of the cast of *Full House* were newcomers to television.

Before being cast as Danny Tanner, the dad in the series, Bob Saget had been a well-known stand-up comic who performed all across America.

Dave Coulier played Joey Gladstone, Danny Tanner's best friend. Like Saget, Coulier was a comedian and was also the set's resident practical joker. "When the girls were 2, I used to flap my arms and tell them, 'If you guys run and flap your arms really fast, you can fly!'" Coulier recalled. "Every day I'd ask, 'Are you guys flying yet?' and they'd say, 'No!'"

John Stamos, who played the girls' Uncle Jesse, became a teen idol to millions of girls while on the show. But to the Olsen girls, he was like a goofy uncle.

Their eldest sister on the show, Donna Jo, or D.J., was played by Candace Cameron. Her older brother Kirk, who appeared on the series *Growing Pains*, was another teen idol.

The part of the middle Tanner daughter, Stephanie, was played by Jodie Sweetin, who was only five years old when the show began. However, unlike Candace Cameron and the Olsen sisters, Jodie decided to quit acting once the series ended. She began attending college at Chapman University in Orange, California, an hour south of Hollywood.

Full House ran for eight years.

Another young actor on the show, Andrea Barber, who played D.J.'s best friend Kimmy, also decided not to pursue acting. After graduating from Whittier College in 1999, she worked for the summer at the United Nations in New York City. Then she got a job as Whittier's assistant director of foreign studies and planned to go back to college to pursue a masters degree in women's rights.

Over the next eight years, Mary-Kate and Ashley would discover that being on a TV series was almost like having two families.

Chapter 3
Home Away from Home

David and Jarnie worried about the girls the longer they were on TV.

Nobody ever imagined that *Full House* would be the smash hit it became, including the cast members. The most surprised people were David and Jarnie Olsen, who never anticipated that their daughters would literally grow up on a television sound stage. But once it became clear that *Full House* was going to be on the air a long time, they did everything they could to make sure Mary-Kate and Ashley kept their feet on the ground. They didn't spoil them and insisted they obey the rules like any other children. So the girls had to have their homework finished before dinner if they wanted to go play afterwards.

"After the first season, we almost pulled them off the show because we worried whether it would be too disruptive to them and to the rest of the family," Dave Olsen admitted. "But Mary-Kate and Ashley really enjoyed being there, and we eventually decided that as long as they were having fun we'd let them keep doing it."

Most child actors work five days a week and are taught exclusively by studio tutors. But Mary-Kate and Ashley worked only three days a week, three weeks a month. The rest of the time they attended a school near their home. "Which is fun, because we got to see our friends," said Mary-Kate, by far the more talkative of the two.

Mary-Kate also revealed that away from the set, the twins are not as inseparable as some might assume. "We do our homework together," she said. "But we have our own friends at school. We sometimes take a break from each other."

"They're regular kids with regular friends who don't treat them any different than anybody else," their dad added. "And it's the same at home."

Their parents weren't the only ones who kept a careful eye on them. So did the rest of the cast. They became a second family to the girls. The closeness of the cast members on *Full House* made it a fun and safe place to

Eventually, they decided that as long as the girls were having fun, they'd let them continue.

grow up. Although everyone worked hard, there was still plenty of time to play and have fun.

In real life, Bob Saget had three daughters of his own so he quickly formed a bond with his TV twins. "They were very sweet, real girlie girls," he recalled. "When I would get them mixed up, I would get the hands on the hips and the 'Don't you know me by now?' look. When their personalities came out more, I started being able to tell them apart. Subtle things, like one was more yuppie and one more Melrose."

In some series, the actors bicker with each other or let petty jealousies cause friction on the set. But the cast of *Full House* enjoyed each other's company. Mary-Kate and Ashley learned that putting on the best show possible was more important than who got to be in the limelight. Lori Loughlin, who played John Stamos' girlfriend and eventual wife on the show, believed that having two grounded parents and a close-knit cast taught the girls how to properly handle fame and celebrity. "We had no prima donnas on the show," Lori said. "I think that helped them become well-rounded people. It's great to see them so successful."

In real life, Bob Saget has three daughters of his own, so he quickly formed a bond with his TV twins.

And they were. By the time they were five years old, Mary-Kate and Ashley were two of the most popular performers on television. Researchers at ABC, the network that aired *Full House*, were astonished to learn

the Olsens had a higher "Q rating"—which is a measure of a star's popularity—among girls than Henry Winkler when he played The Fonz on *Happy Days* or Michael J. Fox when he starred on *Family Ties.*

But the sisters never got big heads, even as their salary kept increasing. The first season they each earned $2,400 per episode. By the

Mary-Kate and Ashley have always been popular actresses among girls.

Mary-Kate and Ashley have grown up in front of a television camera.

final season, they were earning $80,000 an episode. Even so, it was still all about having fun. "I like meeting people, and also going to new places," said Ashley. Mary-Kate added, "We also get to learn new things. It is even fun learning lines."

Even so, the girls continued to live as normal a life as possible. Despite making a lot of money, the girls only got an allowance of $10 a week and were still expected to do chores around the house. As David Olsen once noted, "They work in Hollywood, but they don't live it. They like acting but as soon as they stop enjoying it, it will end."

Chapter 4
In a League of Their Own

One of the first indications that the Olsen sisters had struck a chord with young fans came when a children's publisher called Parachute Publishing put out a paperback book. It was based on an episode of *Full House* that featured Michelle and her older sister Stephanie. The book sold an amazing 70,000 copies. Based on those unexpectedly high sales, the publisher launched a series of books based solely on Michelle.

And there was a lot more than books. The girls' first album, *Brother For Sale,* sold 325,000 copies, while their next project, *Our First Video,* sold 400,000 copies. Then in December 1992, the Olsens' first made-for-television movie, *To Grandmother's House We*

Parachute Publishing launched a series of books based solely on Michelle.

Go, went on the air. It became one of the most watched TV movies of the entire season.

Although Dave and Jarnie had the final say over Mary-Kate and Ashley's career, they wanted some expert guidance. So they hired entertainment attorney Robert Thorne, whose clients included many famous stars.

Because *To Grandmother's House We Go* did so well, Thorne decided it was time to think about the future. He negotiated a development deal with ABC, which means the network promised to create more series and movies for the girls in the future.

"We walked away with a 13-episode series commitment and three telefilms on anything we wanted," Thorne recalled. "That's when I knew. That was the turning point."

It was Thorne who urged the Olsens to form a production company, which would develop other projects for the girls to star in. The company was established in 1993 and was called Dualstar. In the credits for their second TV movie, *Double, Double, Toil and Trouble,* Dualstar was listed as co-producer. That meant that seven-year-old Mary-Kate and Ashley had become two of the youngest producers in Hollywood history.

Thorne urged the Olsens to form a production company, which would develop other projects for the girls to star in.

Thorne was anxious to set up a production company because he knew *Full House* wouldn't be on the air forever. He wanted to be prepared when it came to an end. That finally happened in 1995. But although they were sad to leave their second family, the twins were excited about all the new experiences waiting in front of them.

Mary-Kate and Ashley starred in two successful home video series, The Adventures of Mary-Kate and Ashley *and* You're Invited.

If there was any doubt that Mary-Kate and Ashley were now true Hollywood stars, all anyone had to do was look at their salaries. They earned $125,000 for their first TV movie but by their third, *How the West Was Fun*, their fee had skyrocketed to $1 million. Because their TV movies did so well, both in the ratings and later when released on home video, it only seemed natural that Mary-Kate and Ashley were ready to star in a movie that would appear in theatres.

The film was called *It Takes Two* and had a *Prince and the Pauper* theme with Mary-Kate and Ashley playing a rich girl and a poor girl. They conspire to have their respective guardians, played by Steve Guttenberg and Kirstie Alley, fall in love. The movie cost $14 million to make. Although it only earned $19.5 million at the box office, it amassed over $75 million in home-video retail sales, making it Warner Home Video's fourth-biggest seller ever in the family category.

This was no surprise to the movie's director, Andy Tennant. He still remembers the day when three busloads of kids happened to pass while shooting was taking place. The buses came to an abrupt stop as the kids inside caught site of the Olsens. "Ten minutes later

This photo was taken from the movie, It Takes Two.

there was this stampede of 75 children who had gotten off the bus all screaming," he said. "It looked like the Beatles. They swarmed the set. Everything came to a standstill."

In May 1996, the sisters shared the best actress honor in the Nickelodeon "Kids' Choice Awards" for *It Takes Two*, even beating Alicia Silverstone of *Clueless*. But instead of doing another film right away, the girls decided to concentrate on their two home video series. The first, called *The Adventures of Mary-Kate and Ashley*, is fun mysteries in which the girls play detectives. Mary-Kate starts their motto, "We solve any crime..." and Ashley finishes, "...by dinnertime." The second is a series of party tapes called *You're Invited*.

In 1998, Mary-Kate and Ashley were back on television in the series *Two of a Kind*. On the show, they lived with their single dad, who hires one of his quirky students to take care of them. Unlike *Full House*, each sister got her own role this time so they were very excited about the series. Unfortunately, *Two of a Kind* was canceled after just one season. Although they were disappointed, the girls were hardly at a loss for things to do.

In May 1996, the sisters shared the best actress honor in the Nickel- odeon "Kids' Choice Awards."

Chapter 5
Changing with the Times

In 2000, Mattel introduced fashion dolls of the Olsens.

By 2000, Dualstar was a multimillion-dollar business empire that included over 100 Olsen Twins books, dozens of home videos, game cartridges for Nintendo and PlayStation and their megahit website, www.marykateandashley.com. Yet the girls maintained A averages at the Christian school they attend. "Over the past year, we've been getting more involved," Ashley said about their business dealings. "We're old enough now to understand everything and know what's going on and what should be going on."

Also in 2000, Mattel introduced fashion dolls of the Olsens that are similar to Barbie dolls. "It's kind of weird to have your own doll," said Ashley. "But it's neat too. I dress mine up in clothes like I have at home."

The following year, the girls began a new magazine called marykateandashley. They also launched their own clothing line at Wal-Mart. "It's a little exhausting at times," Mary-Kate admitted, "but it's fun, too."

"Yeah, we're busy," Ashley added. "But we're having a good time and doing a lot of neat stuff. It's fun, getting to see all the cool new clothes in places like Paris. But our favorite shoots have been in Rome and Hawaii, which were both beautiful."

Even though they work so much, Mary-Kate didn't think that they were missing out on regular kid things. "We really do have an advantage over other kids," she said. "We've experienced more than other kids, working how we have."

But their lives haven't always been like a fairy tale. Although most of their classmates like them, the girls admitted that "Some people at school are jealous."

Mary-Kate and Ashley appeared at Barnes & Noble in New York City in 1998 for a book signing of "The New Adventures of Mary-Kate and Ashley."

A more traumatic event occurred when Jarnie and Dave divorced in 1996. It was bad enough that Mary-Kate and Ashley had to deal with their parents splitting up. Then their father remarried a short while later, and the newspapers made it headline news. That caused one of the few major disagreements between the sisters. Mary-Kate attended the wedding ceremony, while Ashley chose to stay home with their mother.

Since then, however, they have adjusted to their dad's new family. Although Ashley and Mary-Kate, along with their brother Trent and younger sister Elizabeth, live with their mother, they see their father regularly. He has two children with his current wife, McKenzie.

Now that they are teenagers, Mary-Kate and Ashley are very mindful of being seen as individuals and not just "the Olsen twins." The girls have very distinct personalities and their own circle of friends. Right-handed Ashley enjoys shopping and being with her friends. Mary-Kate, a leftie, is more the athletic type. She spends a lot of time riding her horse and being outdoors. And as for dressing alike, Mary-Kate wrinkled her nose and said, "That's weird."

What's odd is that the girls have managed to remain as popular as they have for so many years. According to research, they remain the most popular and recognizable young Hollywood stars among American kids, both girls and boys. That probably won't change in the foreseeable future now that they are back on television in a new series called *So Little Time*, which premiered in 2001 on the ABC Family cable channel. In the series they play Riley and Chloe, who divide their time between their divorced parents' homes while also dealing with the daily dramas of high school.

Mary-Kate believes the secret of their enduring success is that kids relate to them. "They feel like they're close to us because they've seen us grow up," she said.

Whether or not both girls, (age 16 in 2002), decide to pursue acting as adults remains to be seen. Ashley seems more committed. "I really like acting," she said. "It's a lot of fun." She's also expressed a desire to be a director.

Mary-Kate may have other aspirations. She's considering going to college to be a veterinarian or training dolphins and whales at Sea World.

But whatever paths the Olsen sisters may take in the future, success seems a foregone conclusion.

Mary-Kate and Ashley are the most popular and recog- nizable young Hollywood stars among American kids.

Chronology

- 1986, born on Friday, June 13th

- 1987, cast in *Full House* when they are seven months old

- 1992, the Olsens' first made-for-television movie, *To Grandmother's House We Go*, goes on the air

- 1993, form Dualstar production company

- 1993, *Mary-Kate and Ashley Olsen: Our First Video* goes to top of Billboard's music video chart in three weeks after release

- 1994, first episode of their video series, *Adventures of Mary-Kate and Ashley: The Case of Thorn Mansion*, makes its debut

- 1995, *Full House* goes off the air

- 1995, first feature film, *It Takes Two*, is released

- 1996, the sisters share the best actress honor in the Nickelodeon "Kids' Choice Awards" for *It Takes Two*

- 1996, parents divorce and father remarries

- 1998, TV series *Two of a Kind* premieres

- 2001, new cable TV series, *So Little Time*, premieres

Filmography

1987 *Full House* (Series)

1992 *To Grandmother's House We Go* (TV Movie)

1993 *Double, Double, Toil and Trouble* (TV Movie)

      Olsen Twins Mother's Day Special (TV)

      How I Spent My Summer Vacation (TV)

1994 *How the West Was Fun* (TV Movie)

      Adventures of Mary-Kate and Ashley: The Case of Thorn Mansion (Video)

      Adventures of Mary-Kate and Ashley: The Case of the Logial I Ranch (Video)

1995 *It Takes Two* (Feature Film)

      You're Invited to Mary-Kate and Ashley's Sleepover Party (Video)

      Adventures of Mary-Kate and Ashley: The Case of the Sea World Adventure (Video)

      Adventures of Mary-Kate and Ashley: The Case of the Mystery Cruise (Video)

      Adventures of Mary-Kate and Ashley: The Case of the Fun House Mystery (Video)

      Adventures of Mary-Kate and Ashley: The Case of the Christmas Caper (Video)

1996 *You're Invited to Mary-Kate and Ashley's Hawaiian Beach Party* (Video)

Adventures of Mary-Kate and Ashley: The Case of the U.S. Space Camp Mission (Video)

Adventures of Mary-Kate and Ashley: The Case of the Shark Encounter (Video)

Adventures of Mary-Kate and Ashley: The Case of the Hotel Who-Done It (Video)

1997 *You're Invited to Mary-Kate and Ashley's New York Ballet Party* (Video)

You're Invited to Mary-Kate and Ashley's Mall of America Party (Video)

You're Invited to Mary-Kate and Ashley's Christmas Party (Video)

You're Invited to Mary-Kate and Ashley's Birthday Party (Video)

Adventures of Mary-Kate and Ashley: The Case of the Volcano Mystery (Video)

Adventures of Mary-Kate and Ashley: The Case of the United States Navy Adventure (Video)

1998 *Two of a Kind* (Series)

Billboard Dad (Video)

You're Invited to Mary-Kate and Ashley's Costume Party (Video)

You're Invited to Mary-Kate and Ashley's Camping Party (Video)

1999 *Passport to Paris* (Video)

Switching Goals (TV Movie)

You're Invited to Mary-Kate and Ashley's Fashion Party (Video)

2000 *Behind the Walls of Full House* (TV)

You're Invited to Mary-Kate and Ashley's School Dance (Video)

You're Invited to Mary-Kate and Ashley's Greatest Parties (Video)

Amazing Adventures of Mary-Kate and Ashley (Video)

2001 *Winning London* (Video)

Fashion Forward: Spring 2001 (TV)

So Little Time (Series)

Index

Alley, Kirstie   22
Barber, Andrea   13
Boyett, Robert   8
Cameron, Candace   13
Coulier, Dave   12
Dualstar   20, 24
Fox, Michael J.   17
Guttenberg, Steve   22
Full House   7, 8, 9, 11, 12, 14, 15, 16, 17, 19, 21
Loughlin, Lori   16
Olsen, David (father)   6, 8, 14, 15, 18, 20
Olsen, Jarnie (mother)   6, 8, 11, 14, 20

Olsen, Mary-Kate and Ashley
   birth of 5
   brothers and sisters 6, 26
   early years 6–23
   education of 24–25
   first start on TV 7–8
   parents of 6, 8, 14, 20
   parents divorce 26
Parachute Publishing   19
Q-rating   17
Saget, Bob   7, 12, 16
Stamos, John   12, 16
Sweetin, Jodie   13
Tennant, Andy   22
Thorne, Robert   20, 21
Winkler, Henry   17